THE ORIGINAL PETER RABBIT BOOKS™

1 The Tale of Peter Rabbit
2 The Tale of Squirrel Nutkin
3 The Tailor of Gloucester
4 The Tale of Benjamin Bunny
5 The Tale of Two Bad Mice
6 The Tale of Mrs. Tiggy-Winkle
7 The Tale of Mr. Jeremy Fisher
8 The Tale of Tom Kitten
9 The Tale of Jemima Puddle-Duck
10 The Tale of The Flopsy Bunnies
11 The Tale of Mrs. Tittlemouse
12 The Tale of Timmy Tiptoes
13 The Tale of Johnny Town-Mouse
14 The Tale of Mr. Tod
15 The Tale of Pigling Bland
16 The Tale of Samuel Whiskers
17 The Tale of The Pie and The Patty-Pan
18 The Tale of Ginger and Pickles
19 The Tale of Little Pig Robinson
20 The Story of A Fierce Bad Rabbit
21 The Story of Miss Moppet
22 Appley Dapply's Nursery Rhymes
23 Cecily Parsley's Nursery Rhymes

Quotes from Beatrix Potter

A Miscellany of Potterisms

The original and authorized edition

FREDERICK WARNE

FREDERICK WARNE

UK | USA | Canada | Ireland | Australia
India | New Zealand | South Africa

Frederick Warne is part of the Penguin Random House group of companies whose addresses can be found at global.penguinrandomhouse.com.

penguin.co.uk   puffin.co.uk   ladybird.co.uk

First published 2016
Some material previously published in *Yours Affectionately, Peter Rabbit*
Frederick Warne & Co. Ltd, 1983
001

Copyright © Frederick Warne & Co. Ltd, 1983, 2016

Peter Rabbit™ & Beatrix Potter™ Frederick Warne & Co.
Frederick Warne & Co. is the owner of all rights, copyrights and trademarks in the Beatrix Potter character names and illustrations

peterrabbit.com

Made and printed in China

A CIP catalogue record for this book is available from the British Library

ISBN: 978–0–241–29007–1

All correspondence to:
Frederick Warne, Penguin Random House Children's,
80 Strand, London WC2R 0RL

Contents

9   Introduction
11 Part One: On Writing
35 Part Two: On Life

INTRODUCTION

Beatrix Potter is an icon. Her charming animal tales have sold millions of copies all around the world, bringing joy to many generations of children and grown-ups. She was a pioneer of her time: a businesswoman who bred prizewinning rare sheep and used the profits from her books to buy up vast tracts of land in the Lake District. This land was donated upon her death to the National Trust.

In addition to her famous Tales, Beatrix also wrote many personal letters, as well as journal entries which were written in code. This code was finally cracked in 1958, fifteen years after her death. Collected here is a miscellany of Potter's opinions about writing and life.

Part One

ON WRITING

> I had thought the book might be in a style between Caldecott & the Baby's Opera; I cannot design pattern borders, but I like drawing flowers.
>
> I will go on with it on approval if you are undecided, or for myself if you decline it; I should not intend sending it to another publisher; but I hope very much you may like the drawings.
>
> I remain, yrs sincerely
> Beatrix Potter

Beatrix Potter is one of the world's most beloved authors. Her stories are read and quoted by children and parents everywhere. Here are some of the most famous lines.

From *The Tale of Peter Rabbit*:

Once upon a time there were four little Rabbits, and their names were – Flopsy, Mopsy, Cotton-tail, and Peter.

From *The Tale of Squirrel Nutkin*:

This is a tale about a tail – a tail that belonged to a little red squirrel, and his name was Nutkin.

From *The Tale of Mr. Tod*:

I have made many books about well-behaved people. Now, for a change, I am going to make a story about two disagreeable people, called Tommy Brock and Mr. Tod.

From *The Tale of Jemima Puddle-Duck*:

Jemima Puddle-duck was a simpleton: not even the mention of sage and onions made her suspicious.

From *The Tale of Mrs. Tiggy-Winkle*:

Why! Mrs. Tiggy-winkle was nothing but a HEDGEHOG.

From *The Tale of The Flopsy Bunnies*:

It is said that the effect of eating too much lettuce is "soporific". I have never felt sleepy after eating lettuces; but then I am not a rabbit.

From *The Tale of Johnny Town-Mouse*:

One place suits one person, another place suits another person. For my part, I prefer to live in the country, like Timmy Willie.

Writing and illustrating a book is never an entirely straightforward exercise, especially when the story is based on real-life animals, people and places.

On writing *The Tale of The Pie and The Patty-Pan*:

I don't think I have ever seriously considered the state of the pie, but the book runs some risk of being over-cooked if it goes on much longer!

To Norman Warne, 6 June 1905

On *The Tailor of Gloucester*:

[This book] has always been my own favourite ... I used to stay with some cousins on the edge of the Cotswolds, overlooking the vale of Severn; they told me the story of the tailor; and I added the mice & the old-fashioned coats.

To Lady Mary Isabel Warren, 23 December 1919

On illustrating hedgehogs for *The Tale of Mrs. Tiggy-Winkle*:

The hedgehog drawings are turning out very comical. I have dressed up a cottonwool dummy figure for convenience of drawing the clothes. It is such a little figure of fun; it terrifies my rabbit.

To Norman Warne, 5 December 1904

Peter Rabbit is Beatrix Potter's most recognizable and successful creation, but she was not overly precious about him.

Before the publication of *The Tale of Peter Rabbit*:

I hope the little book will be a success. There seems to be a great deal of trouble being taken with it.

To Norman Warne, 17 August 1902

On her artistic accomplishments:

*Peter [Rabbit] never aspired to be high art—
he was passable ...*

To Josephine Banner, 28 February 1838

On the origins of Peter:

*I have been asked to tell again how Peter Rabbit
came to be written. It seems a long time ago; and in
another world ...*

To Bertha Mahony Miller, 25 November 1940

Two opinions on the mass appeal of Peter:

I often think that that was the secret of the success of Peter Rabbit, it was written to a child—not made to order.

To Fruing Warne, 26 September 1905

I have never quite understood the secret of Peter's perennial charm. Perhaps it is because he and his little friends keep on their way, busily absorbed in their own doings. They were always independent.

To Bertha Mahony Miller, 25 November 1940

On the cover of *The Tale of Peter Rabbit*:

I do so dislike that idiotic prancing rabbit on the cover!

To Arthur Stephens, 23 February 1941

On the Tale's sixth printing:

The public must be fond of rabbits! What an appalling quantity of Peter.

To Norman Warne, 9 November 1903

On Peter's continuing popularity:

I suppose "Peter" will still be in print in 1907!

To Norman Warne, 4 March 1905

Beatrix loved writing. She had a vivid and extraordinary imagination.

On her urge to create a fantasy world:

I do not remember a time when I did not try to invent and make for myself a fairyland amongst the wild flowers, the animals, fungi, mosses, woods and streams…

To Bertha Mahony Miller, 25 November 1940

Advice for keeping style unsentimental:

My usual way of writing is to scribble, and cut out, and write it again and again. The shorter and plainer the better. And read the Bible (unrevised version and Old Testament) if I feel my style wants chastening.

To Bertha Mahony Miller, May 1929

On the trouble with endings:

I do so hate finishing books. I would like to go on with them for years.

To Norman Warne, 26 June 1905

Beatrix was a keen and accomplished artist, regularly using live models... with varying degrees of success!

On drawing Benjamin Bouncer, a real-life model for her rabbit characters:

My first act was to give Bounce ... a cupful of hemp seeds, the consequence being that when I wanted to draw him next morning he was partially intoxicated and wholly unmanageable.

Journal, May 1890

A bit more background to the characterful Bouncer:

It is interesting about your wild rabbits. I used to tame house mice—so tame that I could pick them up, with food in my hand. But I never had a satisfactory "wild" rabbit... "Peter" was drawn from a very intelligent Belgian hare called Bounce... A noisy cheerful determined animal, inclined to attack strangers.

To Mrs M.C. Grimston, 12 February 1938

A very civilized bunny:

Benjamin was extremely fond of hot buttered toast, he used to hurry into the drawing room when he heard the tea-bell!

Photograph annotation

A bunny with real composure and style:

Benjamin once fell into an aquarium head first, and sat in the water which he could not get out of, pretending to eat a piece of string. Nothing like putting a face upon circumstances.

Journal, 30 October 1892

On the model for Tom Kitten:

I have borrowed a kitten and I am rather glad of the opportunity of working at the drawings. It is very young and pretty and a most fearful pickle. I have not quite finished the kitten. It is an exasperating model.

To Milly Warne, 18 July 1906

On an unfortunate incident involving a guinea pig:

First I borrowed and drew Mr. Chopps. I returned him safely. Then in an evil hour I borrowed a very particular guinea-pig with a long white ruff, known as Queen Elizabeth.

Journal, 30 October 1892

This PIG—offspring of Titwillow the Second, descendant of the Sultan of Zanzibar, and distantly related to a still more illustrious animal named the Light of Asia—this wretched pig took to eating blotting paper, pasteboard, string, and other curious substances, and expired in the night.

Journal, 30 October 1892

On writing *The Tale of Mr. Jeremy Fisher*:

*I have been drawing a frog today with a fishing-rod,
I think it is going to be a funny book.*

To Winifred Warne, 1 December 1905

On an inspiration for (the rather ill-mannered) Squirrel Nutkin:

One day I saw a most comical little squirrel; his tail was only an inch long; but he was so impertinent, he chattered and chattered and threw down acorns onto my head.

To Norah Moore, 25 September 1901

Two insights into the glamorous life of an illustrator:

I spent a very wet hour inside the pig stye drawing the pig. It tries to nibble my boots, which is interrupting ... In the middle of September, I caught myself in the back yard making a careful and admiring copy of the swill bucket.

To Milly Warne, 23 August 1910

Beatrix was a shrewd businesswoman who didn't let her publishers get away with much ...

On the importance – or otherwise – of keeping the reader in mind:

If it were not impertinent to lecture one's publishers—you are a great deal too much afraid of the public; for whom I have never cared one tuppeny-button. I am sure that it is that attitude of mind which has enabled me to keep up the series ...

To Harold Warne, 14 July 1912

On buying books during wartime:

I am surprised and pleased to hear that the books have done so well in these bad times, I expect people want a cheerful present for children, so they buy them.

To Fruing Warne, 18 March 1918

On her work philosophy:

I painted most of the little pictures mainly to please myself. The more spontaneous the pleasure, the more happy the result. I cannot work to order; and when I had nothing to say I had the sense to stop.

To Bertha Mahony Miller, 25 November 1940

On her readers' correspondence:

I have had such comical letters from children about "Scell nuskin"—it seems an impossible word to spell; but they say they have "red" it right through (and that it is "lovely")—which is satisfactory.

To Norman Warne, 8 September 1903

Two thoughts on the value of inexpensive books:

I shall always have a strong preference for cheap books myself—even if they do not pay; all my little friends happen to be shilling people.

To Norman Warne, 8 September 1903

Miss Potter would rather make 2 or 3 little books costing 1/- each, than one big book costing 6/- each, because she thinks little rabbits cannot afford to spend 6 shillings on one book and would never buy it.

To Marjorie Moore, 13 March 1900

On the additional duties of being an author:

I hate publicity; and I have contrived to survive to be an old woman without it...

To John Stone, 19 August 1939

When looking back over her work:

I am very glad the books have given so much pleasure and continue to be useful. I can no longer see to overwork my eyes; and I think I have "done my bit";—unconsciously—trying to copy nature—without affectation or swelled head.

To Janet Adam Smith, 2 February 1943

Part Two
On Life

Beatrix was a devoted pet-owner, and used her many house animals as models for her work. But she was also a farmer and countrywoman, quite unsentimental about animals ...

On unintended house guests:

I seem able to tame any sort of animal; it is sometimes rather awkward on a farm, we cannot keep them out of the house, especially the Puddleducks, and turkeys.

To Eileen Rowson, 6 March 1919

On dogs:

I do not on average care for dogs—especially other people's.

Journal, 31 August 1892

On the character of rabbits:

Rabbits are creatures of warm volatile temperament but shallow and absurdly transparent …

Journal, 30 October 1892

On caring for a lazy rabbit:

My rabbit Peter is so lazy, he lies before the fire in a box, with a little rug. His claws grow too long, quite uncomfortable, so I tried to cut them with scissors but they were so hard that I had to use the big garden scissors.

To Noel Moore, 4 February 1895

On a falling-out:

I had a funny instance of rabbit ferocity last night; I had been playing with the ferret, and then with the rabbit without washing my hands. She, the rabbit, is generally a most affectionate little animal but she simply flew at me, biting my wrists all over before I could fasten the hutch. Our friendship is at present restored with scented soap!

To Norman Warne, September 1903

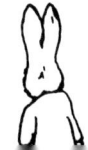

On a new friend:

Bertram went back to school ... leaving me the responsibility of a precious bat. It is a charming little creature, quite tame and apparently happy as long as it has sufficient flies and raw meat. I fancy bats are things most people are pleasingly ignorant about ...

Journal, 16 September 1884

On an unexpected new neighbour:

The Northern suburbs seem to be quite frequently afflicted by raging elephants. The last escaped, jammed itself in a lane where the frightened inhabitants gave it an unlimited supply of buns to keep it from knocking down the houses.

Journal, 26 October 1884

Beatrix took her own education quite seriously, and had many opinions on childhood in general.

On teachers:

A bad or indifferent teacher is worse than none.

Journal, 27 October 1884

On the peculiarities of her education:

Thank goodness my education was neglected; I was never sent to school.

To an American friend, 1929

Of course, what I wore was absurdly uncomfortable; white pique starched frocks just like Tenniel's "Alice in Wonderland", and cotton stockings striped round and round like a zebra's legs.

Essay in *The Horn Book*, May 1929

On "modern" throwaway culture:

I do dislike the modern fashion of giving children heaps of expensive things which they don't look at twice.

To Norman Warne, 8 September 1903

When asked which books she liked to read as a child:

Trash, from the literary point of view—goody-goody, powder-in-the-jam, from the modern standpoint! I liked silly stories about other little girls' doings.

To Mrs Ramsay Duff, June 1943

On art:

It is all the same, drawing, painting, modelling, the irresistible desire to copy any beautiful object which strikes the eye. Why cannot one be content to look at it?

Journal, 4 October 1884

In response to her publishers, when her art was compared to artists she felt were far more accomplished:

Great rubbish, absolute bosh!

To Arthur Stephens, 7 February 1943

Born and raised in London, Beatrix's family often holidayed in Scotland and the Lake District. She was passionate about preserving Britain's environment and wrote beautifully about it.

On her memories of Dalguise, Scotland:

The woods were peopled by the mysterious good folk. The Lords and Ladies of the last century walked with me along the overgrown paths, and picked the old fashioned flowers among the box and rose hedges of the garden... I remember every stone, every tree, the scent of the heather, the music sweetest mortal ears can hear... oh, it was always beautiful, home sweet home.

Journal, 8 May 1884

On the Lakes:

*...sorrows of yesterday, today, and tomorrow;
the vastness of the fells covers all with a mantle of peace.*

The Solitary Mouse

...not even Hitler can damage the fells.

To Margaret Hammond and Cecily Mills, 30 March 1939

Beatrix Potter donated land to the National Trust, both during her lifetime and after her death.

When her identity was revealed after she donated some land anonymously:

The announcement about Thwaite farm, in direct contradiction to my expressed wish, was quite gratuitous … I am very much annoyed about it.

To Mr. S.H. Hamer, 20 July 1932

The Trust is a noble thing, and—humanly speaking—immortal. There are some silly mortals connected with it; but they will pass.

To Bruce Thompson, 23 July 1932

Beatrix's parents were overprotective. It was unusual for an unmarried woman in Victorian times to have such a successful independent career, and the Potters didn't always like it.

To her publisher, Norman Warne, about her father:

...he is sometimes a little difficult. I can, of course, do what I like about the book, being thirty-six.

To Frederick Warne, 22 May 1902

On financial freedoms:

It is something to have a little money to spend on books and to look forward to being independent.

Journal, 14 December 1895

Later in life, Beatrix married William Heelis, a solicitor in the Lake District.

About marriage, she had previously said:

Latter day fate ordains that many women shall be unmarried and self-contained, nor should I personally dream to complain, but I hold an old-fashioned notion that a happy marriage is the crown of a woman's life.

Journal, 1894

Beatrix was a force to be reckoned with in business:

I think I shall attack the County Council about manure. I am entitled to all the road sweepings along my piece, and their old man is using it to fill up holes.

To Milly Warne, 30 September 1906

She had strong opinions:

There are several rows going on! but I am not in any of them at present – though much inclined!

To Millie Warne, 30 September 1906

If the tax is raised, I shall be obliged reluctantly to raise the rent ... I am not a Duke: I bought that field out of my earnings and savings. Also I have no vote!

Leaflet on tax reform, 1910, printed by Martin, Hood & Larkin

It must not be let out the horse leaflet is written by a female.

To Mr. E. Wilfred Evans, 8 March 1910

On farm workers during the war:

I think there will have to be more [women] on the land in the future, but in my opinion they will be ladies [not the] sham "lidies" turned out by the board schools [who] are so despicably afraid of dirtying their hands.

To Augusta Burn, 10 January 1916

Beatrix remembered by a fellow member of a local committee:

She was much loved—also much disliked—but never ignored.

Committee member comments, Hawkshead & District Nursing Association

Even as a young woman, Beatrix was acutely aware of her age. Later on in life, her thoughts often turned to ageing. Well into her seventies she was a remarkably active woman, and still had strong opinions!

On reaching the ripe old age of eighteen:

I am eighteen today. How time does go. I feel as if I had been going on such a time ... what funny notions of life I used to have as a child!

Journal, 28 July 1884

On ageing youthfully:

I feel much younger at thirty than I did at twenty; firmer and stronger both in mind and body.

Journal, 28 July 1896

On the ups and downs of old age:

We all have to go slower as we get older. I am said to have a very strong heart; but I go slowly uphill, physically; and of course downhill in the years.

To Caroline Clark, 19 December 1937

On the benefits of ageing:

I do not resent older age; if it brings slowness it brings experience & weight ... I have felt curiously better & younger these last 12 months.

To Caroline Clark, 8 April 1934

On reaching her final chapters:

I am written out for story books, and my eyes are tired for painting.

To Bertha Mahony Miller, 13 December 1934

Three contemplations on old age:

There is much that us old ones don't like in modern life.

To Joseph Moscrop, 31 January 1936

How strange time is looking back! A great moving creeping closing something closing over one object after another like rising water.

Journal, 26 October 1884

You ask how I like growing old ... I mind it little (with one or two reservations). For one thing to quote a friend "Thank God I have the seeing eye", that is to say, as I lie in bed I can walk step by step on the fells and rough lands seeing every stone and flower and patch of bog and cotton grass where my old legs will never take me again.

To Caroline Clark, 15 February 1937

Quotes Credits

Courtesy Frederick Warne & Co.
Page 16: to Norman Warne, 6 June 1905; page 17: to Norman Warne, 5 December 1904; page 18: to Norman Warne, 17 August 1902; page 21: to Arthur Stephens, 23 February 1941; to Norman Warne, 9 November 1903; to Norman Warne, 4 March 1905; page 23: to Norman Warne, 26 June 1905; page 26: to Milly Warne, 18 July 1906; page 29: to Milly Warne, 23 August 1910; page 30: to Harold Warne, 14 July 1912; page 31: to Fruing Warne, 18 March 1918; page 32 (x2): to Norman Warne, 8 September 1903; page 37: to Norman Warne, September 1903; page 42 to Norman Warne, 8 September 1903; page 43: to Arthur Stephens, 7 February 1943; page 48 to Frederick Warne, 22 May 1902; pages 51 & 52: to Milly Warne, 30 September 1906

Extracts from Beatrix Potter's Journal – page 24: May 1890; pages 26, 27 & 37: 30 October 1892; page 36: 31 August 1892; page 38: 16 September 1884; page 39: 26 October 1884; page 40: 27 October 1884; page 43: 4 October 1884; page 44: 8 May 1884; page 49: 14 December 1895; page 50: 1894; page 56: 28 July 1884; page 57: 28 July 1896; page 61: 26 October 1884

Page 45: Manuscript of *The Solitary Mouse* © Frederick Warne & Co., 1971; page 52: Leaflet on tax reform, 1910, printed by Martin, Hood & Larkin; page 55: committee member comments, Hawkshead & District Nursing Association, taken from *The Tale of Beatrix Potter* by Margaret Lane

Courtesy Victoria and Albert Museum
Page 19: to Josephine Banner, 28 February 1938; page 20: to Fruing Warne, 26 September 1905; page 28: to Norah Moore, 25 September 1901; page 45: to Margaret Hammond and Cecily Mills, 30 March 1939; page 53: to Mr. E. Wilfred Evans, 8 March 1910

Courtesy *The Horn Book*
To Bertha Mahony Miller – pages 19, 20, 22, 23 & 31: 25 November 1940; page 23: May 1929; page 59: 13 December 1934. To an American friend – page 41: 1929. To Mrs Ramsay Duff – page 42: June 1943. Essay in *The Horn Book* – page 41: May 1929

Courtesy Judy Hough
Page 17: to Lady Mary Isabel Warren, 23 December 1919

Courtesy the Free Library of Philadelphia
Page 25: to Mrs M.C. Grimston, 12 February 1938